PRAISE FOR
A

One of the primary tasks of the church is passing on from one generation to the next the Christian message. Too often progressive Christians have faltered in this effort. Fortunately, Bob LaRochelle has written a brief but direct book that speaks to adolescents, respecting their integrity and intelligence. He does this by bringing his broad background in education and ministry, having served as a public high school teacher, a Roman Catholic religious educator, and Protestant pastor, to the conversation. He addresses important theological issues, pointing out differences of understanding, offering his own opinion, but giving plenty of room for discussion. Progressive Christian congregations will find this a helpful and effective resource as it engages in the task of passing on the faith from one generation to the next.

Dr. Bob Cornwall
Author of *Faith in the Public Square,*
Out of the Office: A Theology of Ministry,
and *Unfettered Spirit: Spiritual Gifts for the New Great Awakening*

Christian Faith for Adolescents is a must-read for any teen or adult seeking an introduction to Christianity. LaRochelle masterfully uses his years of expertise working with high school students to deliver a clear and honest description of what it means to be a Christian in each of the major denominations. Instead of spreading personal opinions, this book encourage the reader to meet with religions leaders and find the faith setting that most closely resonates their beliefs. Read. Enjoy. Discover!

Eric R. Hutchinson
Musician/National NonProfit Executive

This is the book that's been missing! With solid content and refreshing candor, Bob LaRochelle has laid out the conversations we all want to have with our teens about faith. His presentation is easy to follow and filled with accessible illustrations and insights. Reflection questions are well-crafted and well-placed – inviting immediate engagement with the issues that impact Christians of any age. This will be my new "go to" resource for teaching Confirmation and more.

Rev. Dr. Karen Bailey-Francois
Pastor, Ellington, CT

CHRISTIAN FAITH FOR ADOLESCENTS

ROBERT LaROCHELLE

Energion Publications
Gonzalez, Florida
2017

ISBN10: 1-63199-435-2
ISBN13: 978-1-63199-435-7
Library of Congress Control Number: 2017949991

Energion Publications
P. O. Box 841
Gonzalez, FL 32560

pubs@energion.com
energion.com

DEDICATION

This book is dedicated to all of the adolescents with whom I have had the opportunity to work over the years. These include the many students I taught in Roman Catholic high schools and all those with whom I ministered in youth programs in several Protestant and Roman Catholic churches. I dedicate this to them with gratitude for the opportunities I had to engage in dialogue with them and to be part of their own personal search for meaning in their lives.

I have written this book in hopes that it can be of help to those who read it and those who work with young people as they seek to internalize and make their own the great resources of the Christian tradition, each in their own context, time and place.

Rev. Dr. Robert R. LaRochelle
Summer 2017

ACKNOWLEDGMENTS

I wish to extend special gratitude to the staff of Energion Publications for their feedback and assistance in the publication of this book. I wish to thank my editor, Chris Eyre, for his thoughtful work and to express my gratitude for the feedback provided by Henry Neufeld, Energion's publisher, and for the outstanding efforts of Jody Neufeld in facilitating the completion of this project.

This book is an attempt to help young people 'engage in conversation' with Christianity. In writing it, I can't help but think of all the adolescents with whom I have had the opportunity to engage in serious discussions about the relevance of the Christian faith in their own lives.

My hope is that this book may make a worthwhile contribution toward meaningful engagement of the Christian community in the task of offering relevant religious education for young people, an education that confronts the deepest questions posed by the very fact that we are alive!

Gratefully,

Dr. Robert R. LaRochelle
Broad Brook, Connecticut
July 2017

FOREWORD

Dear Reader,

Whether you are reading this because you are required to, or because you were curious about the title, or because you were persuaded to do so, I hope it will provide you with answers about the faith which you are about to affirm or investigate further.

This book is aimed at you as you explore the area of religion and religious faith. It would interest me greatly if you would share your experiences and thoughts about this book with me by either emailing me at rpbksl@gmail.com or posting on my blog at www.pastorbobsw.blogspot.com . Your feedback is important to me. I want to get a sense of how you, the reader, related to this book and whether you have found it useful to you in exploring this topic of religious faith.

You may be reading as part of a group, or as recommended by a pastor or teacher. Actually, I would recommend that you do read it this way, as the chapters have a set of questions to consider, and it is always better to do this with someone else. If so, you should take part in conversation with your group and your group leader. If you are reading this on your own, I suggest considering finding at least one person with whom you can talk about this book and with whom you can share your ideas.

At the end of the book are some suggestions for further reading, but other group members or your leader will have their own suggestions – I hope you will want to investigate further!

Pastor Bob

ABOUT THE AUTHOR

For many years now, I have been a pastor in different Christian churches. However, that is not something that just happened. The questions I asked and the choices I made as a teenager contributed to what became a career decision. When I was a teenager, I asked a lot of questions and found myself challenging many aspects of the faith in which I was raised. Somewhere along the line I read a passage from a poet that expressed so well what was going on inside of me at the time: 'Be patient toward all that is unsolved in your heart and try to love the questions themselves.' It was that realization that being connected to a religious faith entailed and embraced an attitude of 'loving the questions' that made so profound a difference in my life.

As I write this book, I am serving as a pastor in a Lutheran Church and before that, I did the same in two churches known as Congregational, part of the denomination called the United Church of Christ. For many years before that, I held positions of leadership within the Roman Catholic Church.

I have taught high school religion classes in Catholic schools, headed up programs for youth in local churches, done over a hundred youth retreats, many of which were overnight ones. In addition, I have worked in schools as a Counselor and, for a long time, was a basketball and baseball coach. I have been married for thirty-six years and have three adult children and a brand new granddaughter! So, yes, I guess you could call me 'old,' right?

In all of those years working in these different Christian churches I have spent a lot of time and energy working with young people- and I have loved it!

I'm now hoping to bring some of that experience to you, even though I'm not "your" pastor or youth leader. Please feel free to share your feedback by contacting me or by posting on social media. If you find this book helpful to you, I hope you will consider sharing it with others and engaging in conversations with them as well.

TABLE OF CONTENTS

CHAPTER ONE

WHY ARE YOU READING THIS BOOK?

I am writing this thinking mainly of people who are going through a Confirmation or Baptism preparation program in a church.

Yet, it is also possible that you are reading this as someone who has had no education in any Christian church. Maybe you have friends who have gone to Sunday School and other church classes, but that experience has not been a part of your life.

You may very well be curious about what your friends are doing and talking about when they go to church. It is possible that you might even be considering checking it out someday yourself. You might even be very close to making plans to attend a church service fairly soon.

I suspect that some of you reading this are really skeptical about and suspicious of religion. You have seen evidence on television and social media about the ways in which religious leaders and members of Christian churches have not always been the kindest, most tolerant folks you have ever met. You have been exposed to all kinds of historical information which makes it pretty clear that religion has oftentimes been a force promoting division and hatred. You know about wars that have been fought over religious ideas and you see an abundance of evidence about religious leaders behaving badly and religious groups making life difficult for people who are 'different'. As a matter of fact, you may see this designation of 'difference' as a problem in itself, a problem sadly all too often promoted by those who speak in the name of religion. I hope that this book will go some way towards convincing you that not all of Christianity is the same.

This book is intended as an overview of Christianity. It is not intended to be a book that teaches you the specific teachings of any particular church (such as whichever church you may be thinking of joining).

What do I mean?

Different churches within Christianity have particular teachings and rules and regulations that are specific to that church. These are things that will be addressed directly by your teachers and other church leaders. For example, even though all Christians share in this experience called 'Communion', what Communion means is understood differently by various churches, and while I will make reference to some of those differences, if you are reading as part of a program, your group leader will spell out for you how this teaching is viewed in your particular church that happens to be using this book.

Did you know?
There are over 33,000 different organizations which are in some sense Christian churches. They are usually referred to as "denominations." They range in size from over a billion to a few thousand members.

I will talk about some of the differences between the main denominations later, but do not want this to get in the way of describing Christianity for you.

I am therefore going to deal only with things which are common to all (or at least most) churches. I intend to walk you through some of the basics of Christianity, such as why it exists, how it developed and what it stands for, while, at the same time recognizing that there are those who interpret Christianity differently from others who also call themselves Christian. In other words, there is a lot of disagreement within Christianity about what Christianity is supposed to stand for.

For those who are not part of a church yet, but are curious, I would encourage you to look for opportunities offered in your area by churches whose approach to Christian faith you might see as resonating with your own. You may want to do what I did as a young person and make some appointments with different ministers and priests, representatives of different churches, and ask questions of them that you find important and interesting in your own personal quest!

I really want to spend time helping you explore the heart of what makes up the kind of faith we describe as 'Christian'. In other words, I am interested in getting you to look at what it is that all of these churches which go by different names but all agree that they are Christian churches, really have in common with one another.

I believe that asking 'religious' questions is important. Actually, I believe that all of us, regardless of our age, have all kinds of questions stirring up in our minds and that it is important to both think about and discuss them.

I also believe that, throughout history, religion has been a source and inspiration for both good and evil. Of course, I believe that it should be for good, but I also recognize that, as we attempt to work for a better, more peaceful world, we need what has been described as 'religious literacy.' In other words, we need people who understand enough about the history of religion that they are able to understand that even when religion is used for evil purposes, there is much more to religion than its often inappropriate use.

For better and for worse, Christianity has been a powerful force in the history of the world. I believe that young people with whom I have worked deserve a fair, direct and honest exposure to what Christianity is and to what it is not.

All of us, regardless of our age, share a common humanity and in this humanity, we know that we have a lot of questions, serious questions, about some of the most important things in life. My contention is that no matter how intelligent or well read a person is, there is a lot we do not know about some of the greatest mysteries of life. Young people and adults alike share in the same human condition. In a very real sense, we are all seekers, seeking answers and grappling with questions about some of the great mysteries that constitute our lives. Therefore, while this book is aimed at young people, I think people older than you are, including your teachers, might find it useful too!

As we begin this journey through the pages of this short book, I encourage you to look at these questions, to think about them and discuss them, perhaps with the group with whom you are reading this book or with friends or family on your own. After you talk about them or, if you cannot find time to talk, after you give them serious thought, we will move on and we will try to look realistically at what it means to look at this topic of Christianity from right where you are at this point in your life.

REFLECTION AND DISCUSSION QUESTIONS

(I hope you will want to discuss the topics in each chapter with your group, with friends or with the person who recommended the book to you. These questions and those in the other chapters are intended to help start the conversation)

1. What words would you use to describe your religious affiliation? (Some options include: believer, unbeliever, searcher, skeptic, Catholic, Protestant, Baptist, agnostic, atheist – and there are many more)
2. Explain why you chose the words that you did.

CHAPTER TWO

BEING AN ADOLESCENT:

PLACING RELIGION IN THE CONTEXT OF YOUR OVERALL LIFE

This book you are reading is intended to be read by people who share the common bond of going through adolescence. Using school categories the way they are used in the United States, this means people who are of middle school (some places still call it 'junior high') or high school age. Those of you in high school would more than likely say that your concerns are somewhat different from what they were in middle school or junior high. On the other hand, if you are on the younger side of this age range, you would more than likely see that in many ways your life is evolving differently from how it did when you were, say, a first grader. You might even look ahead to what your life is going to be like in just a few years, when you are in high school.

There are people who study this period of adolescence for a living. People have spent a good deal of time studying "adolescent psychology" in college or graduate school. Actually, a lot of people who work with you in your school have taken courses on this subject. Those professionals who work with you, i.e. your teachers, administrators and counselors, as part of their training, have had to pay attention to the fact that your 'stage' of life, as with any other stage, has its own unique challenges, as well as its own unique joys.

Those who have studied "adolescent psychology" will have encountered the writings of Erik Erikson. He was a psychologist who wrote a great deal about what he had observed about people as they moved through the different ages and stages of their lives. For example, he wrote about babies and how they should be treated. He concluded that, if things went very well, if a baby had his or her basic needs for food and comfort met, that child would develop a sense of TRUST which could carry him or her along as they moved on to confront other challenges in this lives.

Erikson identified eight basic stages in life which we all go through:

Stage	Psychosocial Crisis	Basic Virtue	Age
1	Trust vs. mistrust	Hope	Infancy (0 to 1½)
2	Autonomy vs. shame	Will	Early Childhood (1½ to 3)
3	Initiative vs. guilt	Purpose	Play Age (3 to 5)
4	Industry vs. Inferiority	Competency	School Age (5 to 12)
5	Ego identity vs. Role Confusion	Fidelity	Adolescence (12 to 18)
6	Intimacy vs. isolation	Love	Young Adult (18 to 40)
7	Generativity vs. stagnation	Care	Adulthood (40 to 65)
8	Ego integrity vs. despair	Wisdom	Maturity (65+)

Erikson wrote of adolescence that the major task of this period YOU are going through is to emerge with a solid sense of IDENTITY, that is, a sense of WHO you are. Now, if you are reading this and saying 'I already know who I am', an adolescent psychologist might say that much of how you identify yourself comes from how you have been defined throughout your life. In other words, your parents and other significant others, have passed on to you their expectations about how they want you to behave and often think. During "adolescence", your brain and your body change in significant ways and you are prone to asking a lot of questions, questions that are often on a pretty deep level. One of the outcomes of asking questions is that you could find yourself challenging some of the basic assumptions found in what you have been taught.

It's not unusual for parents and others close to you to say that they notice changes in the ways you accept things that are told you, by noting the situations where you don't accept the things that are told you. That is because your minds are developing and also because your bodies may very well be also. Somewhere during this time frame, not necessarily at the same time for everyone, comes the emergence of sexual feelings. Sexual feelings often lead to decisions centered around what to do with them, including where they fit in to relationships that are part of your life.

At this point, you might be saying 'But isn't this a book about religion??' Well, yes it is, and what is important to point out is that as the mind develops, people start thinking about new questions about what we might call 'much deeper things'. People are less likely to accept on the surface answers they have been told about those things over the course of their lives. People become more likely to try to think for themselves. I would imagine that many readers of this book have been told throughout their lives that they are expected to go to church or Sunday School on Sundays. At a certain point in their lives, many young people challenge and ask 'why?' In addition, having new experiences, such as emerging sexual feelings, brings with it new questions of what is right and what is wrong in terms of sexual behavior. These are questions people just don't have to confront when they are younger.

Likewise, these new experiences and feelings, coupled with the continued emerging growth of your brain, may lead you to raise some questions about things you have traditionally been taught or cause you to look at issues about which you have never really thought before. Most seven or eight year olds don't really ponder the right or wrong of certain sexual activity, right? That is just not part of their experience or what we might call their 'frame of reference.' However, we have to be clear: These changes are not simply limited to sex, although human sexuality is a very powerful reality in the lives of human beings, for sure!

As we grow up, we are capable, because of our intellectual growth, of looking more independently at a lot of things in life. We discover that there are many things about which we have to make decisions and that often these are decisions about what is right and what is wrong. In addition, we recognize perhaps that there are a lot of different ways of looking at a variety of issues and that not everyone looks at things the same way. You might recognize that making decisions is not always a clear and easy thing!

This is a period in peoples' lives where, if they have been raised in a home where they have been expected to attend church or go to religious education classes, such as the one you may now be in, it is not unusual to start questioning some of what you have been taught- about the Bible, the church or what makes up right or wrong.

I will be honest with you: Some adults in churches absolutely hate that! Their idea of 'religious education' is to be sure you have all the 'right answers'. The problem, from my point of view, is that some of those 'right answers' may not sit too well with the way your mind is developing. They may make no sense scientifically or even on a gut emotional level. You may find yourself asking all kinds of questions about the Bible, for example and not be terribly pleased with the answers you are getting:

' Yes, the world was created in six days'...

'But, why? …'

'Because it says so in the Bible …'

A particularly unhelpful answer which some people give is: ' God didn't make Adam and Steve. He made Adam and Eve …'

By the way, you might wonder, why are you calling God 'He'?

I have also found that this period of adolescence is a time when many young people who have not been raised in 'religiously based' homes find themselves intrigued by religious questions. They are often interested in why, for some of their friends, going to church services or youth group is important and means a lot to them, or why, for others, this isn't the case.

So, what I am really saying to you here, is that 'religious' questions are really important questions for someone your age and here is why I think that they are:

Religion is really about dealing with life's mysteries.

You will read more about that in the next chapter. And, as a young person whose mind is developing and who is experiencing things in life you did not experience when you were six or eight, so much of what you are doing in life is really about what all of us adults have to do—you are trying to make some sense out of the mystery. You are trying to find a way to walk through life which makes sense to you, answers your deepest questions and brings you joy, happiness and hope. You are doing what all of us need to do regardless of our age, but the process of doing so might seem to be so powerful a force in your life because it represents a change from one stage of your life into another. It is the movement, really, from childhood into adulthood- and it is not always easy!

What I am saying is not that you leave 'teenage hood' with an identity that can never grow or develop, but that it is a great time to plunge ever more deeply into the great mysteries of life - and it is the great mysteries of life that makes up the very reason there is such a thing as 'religion' at all.

Let's move on … and look at this together.

REFLECTION AND DISCUSSION QUESTIONS

1. What do you see as changes that occur between childhood and adolescence?

2. Have any of your 'religious views' changed throughout your life? Which ones? How?

3. What do you think of the whole idea of 'stages in life?'

4. What are the most fundamental questions you have to which you would like answers? Write these down and hang onto them during the rest of this course, and see how many of them are answered.

CHAPTER THREE

WHAT IS RELIGION?

I am going to start this chapter by asking you to define the word religion. I am not asking you to look it up in a dictionary. Instead, I am suggesting that you say (or think of) what comes to your mind when you hear that word. In fact, if you are reading this book in a class right now, I will also ask you to close the book and have a discussion about this before you read any further in this chapter. And, if you are not in class, to simply put the book down and think. In either situation, then, what comes into your mind when you think of the word "religion"?

When you come back to the book ...

I think that when people talk about "religion," they oftentimes think about the names of religions or churches. They might identify religion with Catholic, Christian, Jewish, Muslim and so on. They might even call people "religious" because they know these people go to church or temple or mosque or pray, or otherwise do "religious" things. What I would like to introduce to you right now is a different way of defining religion. It is something I learned from a writer who wrote religion textbooks, including one I used when teaching a high school religion class many, many years ago.

Here is the best definition of religion that I know:

Religion is our personal response to the mystery of life.

Let me break this down a little bit: First of all, religion is PERSONAL. In other words, even if both of us belong to the same church, you and I respond to life differently. We each have our own unique ways of looking at things, don't we? If you put two people side by side and asked the question: 'Do you believe in God?' and they both said 'yes' and then you followed up with the question 'OK, tell me about God,' I would suspect that you would get some differences in their two definitions or descriptions. One might say 'I see God as my Father'; another, 'God is this source of life I feel within me,' maybe not even a 'person,' more like well 'a force' or 'a feeling.' They both believe in God, right? But there are differences!

A writer I like, who happened to be a minister in a church in New York City, Forrest Church, used to say that when people told him they did not believe in God, he would often say to them 'OK, tell me about the God you don't believe in.' Church (pretty good name for a minister, right?) said that he would often find himself in agreement, even though this pastor believed in 'God.' He would say that he'd find himself saying quite often that 'I don't believe in that kind of a God either.' In other words, the word 'God' can mean different things to different people.

So, what I am trying to tell you is that, really, if you think about it, religion is a personal response to the fact that we live in mystery.

By "mystery" I do not mean "who shot JFK" or even "which came first, the chicken or the egg." I mean the really basic mysteries, such as "Why is there something rather than nothing?" or "Why do bad things happen to good people?" (the second is actually the inspiration behind an excellent book by Rabbi Harold Kushner, *When Bad Things Happen to Good People*)

If we did not live in mystery, there would not be so many opinions out there in the world, would there be? What I want to suggest to you is that if you and I were to take a good look at everything that is mysterious in life, what we would come up with would most likely fall into three basic categories: MYSTERIES OF ORIGIN, MYSTERIES OF DESTINY, and MYSTERIES OF MEANING.

Let's break this down and within the breakdown, let's see how different people respond to mystery:

MYSTERIES OF ORIGIN

I think that if left to our own devices and asked to name the things we wonder about, I think a lot of us would say that we wonder about how the world ever began. We were not there so we do not have first-hand knowledge, right? Over the history of human beings on this planet, people have come up with all kinds of answers. A common one is: God made the world. Others leave God out and argue for a 'Big Bang'. Still others counter that a 'Big Bang' does not account for how the elements within the bang got there. Some say that it all happened in six days as it says in the Book of Genesis in the Bible. Others quarrel with what the word 'day' means in the Bible.

Did you know?

The term "Big Bang" was actually coined by a Jesuit priest who was a scientist, Fr. Lemaitre — who definitely didn't think he was "leaving God out of it." Many scientists think the Big Bang is HOW God created.

Even those who believe God created the world have different theories: Did He create the world in His mind and allow it to evolve (and why say "His"...and what do we mean by mind? Does God have a mind like ours?). Is God's hand (What do we mean by hand?) in the continued evolution of the world and universe? If the answer to that question is yes, then it begs another question, exactly how did God do that? Where does human freedom come into play? If God knows all, as many believe, in what sense are people truly free?

As you can see, people respond to that mystery in different ways. We respond personally, even when we are in general agreement with others. Even with respect to our personal beginnings, there are different ways of looking at the involvement of 'God' in that process, right? Did God intend for you to exist? Were you 'in God's mind' from the beginning of time? As you can see, there are a lot of questions here — and people do have different answers! Even people who agree on the same language have nuances of difference in terms of their interpretation and use of language.

MYSTERIES OF DESTINY

We wonder: Where are we headed? As individuals, is there life after death? What will that be like? Will we see and relate to others? All kinds of different theories and religions have centered around these questions and many people have constructed often complicated answers to them, as well as what seems to others to be far too simple explanations.

Some believe in predestination, others reincarnation. Some believe that our souls come back in other bodies. Others say we just die. Still others that there will be a future reign of God on earth. There is often a strong connection between how we approach destiny and where we find meaning. In extreme form, consider Billy Joel's song *Only the Good Die Young*:

> They say there's a heaven for those who wait.
> Some say it's better, but I say it ain't.
> I'd rather laugh with the sinners than cry with the saints.
> The sinners are much more fun.
> and only the good die young!

In the lyric of that song, you can sense the writer's connection of destiny and meaning. If there is no heaven, some might say, and that is what we are working for, why are we depriving ourselves of fun in this life in pursuit of something that may not exist? Now, I don't accept that thinking for a lot of reasons, but I think you can see in it how there is a connection between how we see our destiny and the meaning we attach to how we act here upon this earth!

MYSTERIES OF MEANING

People hold different opinions on what gives meaning and purpose to life. Ask many Christians and they will tell you 'the teachings of Jesus.' Those of Jewish faith would speak of 'the law and the prophets.' You would hear others affirm the teachings of Muhammad or the Buddha. Still others, who could be called existentialists, would argue that they construct their own meaning in life.

> **"Existentialist" is a name given to people, usually philosophers or theologians, who concern themselves with the questions "Why is there something rather than nothing?" and "What is the meaning of life?"**

If you think about it, there really is a distinction between creating meaning and discovering it, isn't there? If we discover meaning, what is implied is that there is some built in meaning that is not always clear, but it really is there! If we create meaning, we would say that whatever meaning is, is not universal for everyone, but rather is something that I have found gives meaning to me. My meaning may not be yours.

If you are finding this all confusing and even wondering why you are reading this in a Christian Education or Sunday School class, let me pause right here and speak to that possible question of yours:

In looking at Christian faith and the faith as expressed in different Christian churches, what is really important is to see how

Christianity responds to questions that all of us human beings really share in common. THAT IS REALLY THE HEART AND THE PURPOSE OF WHAT I AM TRYING TO SHARE WITH YOU IN THIS CHAPTER!

What I am saying is that, in a very real way, for one who has chosen Christianity, Christian faith provides a personal response to the great mysteries of life, mysteries all people must encounter. Yet, what we will also see as we continue along in this book, is that within Christianity there are different responses and also different ways of looking at those who don't identify their personal response as 'Christian.'

In the next chapter, we are going to look at where Christianity fits into all of this. Before you get there, I want you and those in your class (if you are reading this in a group) to explore the following questions. If you are not in a class, think through them on your own and also find someone with whom you can discuss them as well.

QUESTIONS FOR DISCUSSION:

1. What do you think of as "religion"? Is it similar to the author's definition of religion?
2. What do you see as some of life's greatest mysteries?
3. How do your personal beliefs give answers to any of life's mysteries?
4. What questions of origin, destiny and meaning do you find most difficult for you to understand?
5. Consider and discuss the difference between creating and discovering meaning.
6. Where does your view of Jesus fit into all of this? (You can discuss this now, but you may also want to hold off until you read the next chapter).

CHAPTER FOUR

WHERE DOES CHRISTIANITY FIT IN?

Remember what we said in the last chapter: When we are talking about religion, we are discussing the different responses that people have to the mystery of life. When we look at different well-known responses, we think of a variety of organized religious groups and then we consider different religious approaches. Actually, let's start at looking at the question of religious approaches. An approach to religion takes into account where an individual person happened to stand on the biggest question of them all- is there or is there not a reality beyond that which is human, i.e. does 'the divine' exist? Simply put: IS THERE A GOD?

When you think about an approach to religion, you find three distinct categories:

1. The BELIEVER – This is a person who believes that there is such a reality as God or some kind of spiritual force or presence. In some traditions, this may be several different gods (polytheism). In others, such as Christianity, Judaism and Islam, it would mean ONE God (monotheism).

2. The ATHEIST – This is someone who denies the existence of 'the divine', i.e. a God, gods or some other spiritual presence. You could say that just as the believer places faith in the divine, the atheist places faith that there is no real world of the spirit.

3. The AGNOSTIC – This is an individual who, while open to other possibilities, simply cannot say 'Yes, I believe in God (the divine)' and is able to categorize her/himself as one whose consistent approach is to say simply 'I don't know.'

Now, within the category of 'the believer,' you have many variations. This would include Hindus, Muslims, Jews, and those who are adherents of a wide variety of religions of various organizational structures. Within some traditions, as an example, Buddhism or Unitarianism, you have a variety of different beliefs regarding the actual existence of the divine.

Can this get complicated? YOU BET! That is why simplifying religion and religious questions does no justice to the seriousness of what is being considered in those questions!

Now, within this category of believer, as I mentioned above, we find those who call themselves Christian. Generally speaking, Christians fall in three basic categories:

Within each of these groups, there are variations, but here is as simple a breakdown as I can possibly give:

---

1. ROMAN CATHOLIC CHRISTIANS

2. ORTHODOX CHRISTIANS

3. PROTESTANT CHRISTIANS

ROMAN CATHOLICISM refers to the church of which the Bishop of Rome (Pope) is recognized as the head.

ORTHODOX CHRISTIANITY – What we call Orthodox Churches are the result of disagreements that took place within the church before the eleventh century over some beliefs, including the role of the Pope. There are several churches within this grouping, but the largest are the Greek Orthodox and the Russian Orthodox.

PROTESTANT CHRISTIANITY represents churches that broke from Roman Catholicism largely in the 16th century Reformation and current church communities that do not recognize the authority of the Pope as head of their church. Some Protestants would also trace their ancestry back even prior to the Reformation, rooted in ideas expressed by those who questioned some of the underlying assumptions around which Catholicism was structured.

If you are reading this book as part of a class in a church, it is important that you acquire a working knowledge of where your own church fits into this overall picture. If you are in the United States or Canada and your church is part of the Protestant Christian tradition, you could be part of any one of a large number of what we call 'denominations' or 'brands' of Protestant Christianity. A very incomplete list would include the following: Anglicans, Episcopalians, Lutherans, Methodists, Baptists, Presbyterians, Congregationalists, Evangelicals, Pentecostal. The list goes on and on. In fact, as a class activity, I would encourage you to go to an online encyclopedia and look up 'denominations.'

However, regardless of where your church fits into this breakdown of Christian churches, as part of a Christian church you hold several things in common with other Christian churches. Here is a listing of some of the most important beliefs you share. These are solid points of agreement between your church and the churches of others who call themselves Christian. Having said this, there are some groups who call themselves Christian who would say that, while they don't necessarily believe everything listed below, they DO, quite comfortably, self identify as Christian. However, I think it is fair to say that these beliefs constitute the core of commonly held Christian belief:

Commonly Held Christian Beliefs

1. God exists.
2. God was revealed in Jesus and is experienced as Creator, Christ and Holy Spirit, traditionally referred to as Father, Son and Holy Spirit.
3. Jesus was a great teacher.
4. Jesus called people to 'follow him.' Over time, this evolved into what we call 'church.'
5. Jesus was crucified yet was victorious over death.
6. The 'Easter event' is pivotal in Christian faith.
7. It is important for Christians to worship together.
8. Baptism and Communion (known as 'sacraments') are to be shared by Christian communities.
9. Service to others, especially those in need, is essential to Christian faith.
10. Eternal life is linked to the 'Jesus event' (by which I mean the whole of the impact upon the world of Jesus, before, during or after his actual lifetime).

I would be lying to you if I told you that all Christians or all denominations interpret these common core beliefs in exactly the same way. Likewise, the same for how people worship. If you were to walk into different Christian churches on Sunday morning or on a Saturday for those churches who worship then, something I suggest you consider doing, you would find all kind of different styles of worship:

In some, leaders would wear fancy robes. In others, casual dress.

In some, you would hear older, traditional music. In others, Christian rock.

In some churches, people would worship with set responses in a worship book. In others, people would pray and respond to worship with great emotion and spontaneity.

Some would offer communion every week; others, once a month or less.

In some churches, you'd kneel for Communion. In others, you would stand. In still others, you would sit.

Yet, even more so, you would find even deeper differences:

1. **Some preachers would tell you that the Bible is to be 'believed' word for word. Others would emphasize the symbolic value or the lesson behind it.**
2. **In some, you might hear that homosexual behavior or remarriage after divorce are wrong and that some people present there would not be able to receive Communion because they are divorced and remarried without having an annulment. Other Christian churches would say that 'all are welcome' in their congregation and at the Communion table.**
3. **In some churches, women would lead worship and preach. In others, only men.**
4. **Some would encourage conservative political involvement. In other churches, you would hear more of a liberal agenda. Still others would try to avoid politics whatsoever.**

In these next few pages, I am going to attempt to provide you an overview of what I would call the core of Christianity. I will attempt to tell you as much as I can in as few words as possible about what I know about Jesus, where He came from and what he taught. I will try to identify the heart of soul of Christian faith and why I 'follow Him.'

As I do so, there may be those who would read my words who will tell you that I am missing the point and that I am emphasizing certain things about Jesus and playing down other important beliefs. What you are about to read is not the ultimate, definitive word about Jesus. ***What I want it to be is a starting point for you to consider and for you to discuss.***

Depending upon your denomination or your local church, what I write will most likely be supplemented by some of the great books that have come out of your denomination's history. For example, I am a pastor in a Lutheran church. If I were using this book in a class, I would also be sure to have my students read Martin Luther's *The Small Catechism*, a little book that has long defined the essentials of Lutheran Christianity. (Other denominations and churches have catechisms that serve the same function in their traditions.)

However you use this little book you are reading in relation to other resources, I hope you find the following helpful!

JESUS

It is a commonly accepted fact among those who study history that the man Jesus is one of the most important figures in world history. In writing this, I am simply stating a historical fact. While people may differ about who Jesus is, most will acknowledge his importance and influence. A basic fact about Jesus is that those who became his followers signed on to a movement that would have major influence throughout the world.

For a few moments, let's put out of our minds any questions about the 'religious' meaning of who Jesus was/is and what his

teachings are about. Let's consider a few simple facts that indicate
how the religion centered around faith in him has influenced world
culture. From your study of history, you know about how Christianity spread throughout Europe and how some of the biggest
political battles in the history of the world centered around the
Christian religion. I am referring here to such events as the Reformation and the Great Schism.

In addition to this, I am sure you are well aware of the incredible architectural wonders of the world such as the great cathedrals
in Europe (Notre Dame in Paris is but one example) that were built
by followers of the Christian religion. Think of all of the famous
colleges, places like Harvard and Yale, Wheaton in Illinois, St. Olaf,
Notre Dame, Georgetown, Boston College, Holy Cross and Gon-
zaga and all of the well known hospitals that were founded and
built by followers of the Christian faith. The Christian influence
in the thinking and writing of many of the founders of the United
States is well documented, though their specific viewpoints were
really more diverse than often acknowledged. Many great cities
were named after people who were known for their adherence to
Christianity. Virtually every city with a saint in front of it has such
a background and even some countries, one example being El Salvador ('The Savior,' a reference to Jesus).

Now before we go into some specifics about Jesus, I have to
make a disclaimer: In stating some 'facts' about Jesus, some readers might say that I have left some things out. You see, what I am
attempting to do here is to give you an overview about this man
Jesus. I am not taking it a step further and stating absolutely what
all of this might mean. In other words, in this chapter you won't
see me trying to convince you to 'believe in' Jesus, even though I
will most gladly say that I do. What I am trying to do is to do my
best to lay out some facts, information you can find in the gospels
of Matthew, Mark, Luke and John in the Bible. We can and will
move into some interpretations of all of this later. So, with all of
that in mind, here goes:

- Jesus was raised in what we identify as the Jewish faith.
- His mother was Mary.
- He grew up in a fairly insignificant and isolated town named Nazareth.
- When he reached about thirty years old, he sensed a new direction for his life.
- He began to travel throughout the region we now call Israel. Along the way, he invited others to join him and to be his disciples.
- According to written reports, he made himself very available to people who were considered outcasts- sinners, women, prostitutes, foreigners and even the despised Romans of his day.
- His teaching emphasized the Kingdom (reign) of God—a world in which God's love was present in the way people treated each other. It also contained a powerful message of judgment for those who would not adjust and change their ways as needed.
- He irritated many religious leaders of his day as he taught a message that some would consider quite radical. He questioned the emphasis religious people gave to 'legalism,' at one point saying that even the sacred Sabbath law is made for human beings, not the other way around.
- This irritation turned to outright hostility and people set out to silence him.
- He eventually was crucified on a day now called 'Good Friday.' The night before he died, he gathered his closest friends together for a final meal. Many who study his life would say that it was the meal of the Jewish Passover. At that meal, he shared bread and wine and identified those elements with himself.
- Not long after he died, reports began to spread that he really was alive. In books that would eventually be written about him (known as the Gospels), we find some variety in those appearances.
- Those who were his followers (disciples) who experienced this 'Easter event' became filled with a deep commitment to get the word out about him, even as they recognized that he was not to be among them physically as the Gospels also acknowledge that he was not to be found physically here upon this earth.

THE GOSPELS

The Bible contains four books that deal specifically with the life and teachings of Jesus. These are the Gospels of Matthew, Mark, Luke and John. These books are not really biographies. If you are looking for all kinds of details about specifics of his life, you certainly won't find them here. Yet, what is preserved in these really important books is a lot of valuable information:

- Background about his religious influences, including his references to parts of the Jewish Bible that were really important to him. When you can, check out Luke, Chapter 4. This records his appearance reading the Hebrew Scriptures in the synagogue and identifying himself with this passage.
- Many stories that he told including an incredible collection of parables. For a great example of this, read the three parables found in Luke 15. This section contains my personal favorite, the parable of the Prodigal Son. An interesting exercise I sometimes set is to read this parable slowly while playing the Eagles song "Desperado" in the background. Why not try this?
- The different ways in which he healed people, both physically and simply by the way he treated them. Reports of healing were quite typical in those days when referring to people who were held in high esteem as messengers of God. Jesus was not alone in being referred to as a healer. Oftentimes, these stories are used by some Christians as proof of divinity. It needs to be said that Jesus was not the only one who was claimed to have such 'powers.'
- The Sermon on the Mount found in Matthew 5-7, an incredible collection of teachings centered around how we should live our lives.

THE DEVELOPMENT OF CHRISTIANITY

What you will also find in the Bible both in these Gospels and in the other twenty-three books in what is called the New Testament is an interesting mix of beliefs about Jesus. Oftentimes these beliefs as expressed by the writers of these documents provide the backdrop for the teaching of Jesus that is cited within the Gospel document. There are examples of this everywhere in the New Testament, but as good an example as I can give is to encourage you to read through many of the 'I Am' statements Jesus makes as recorded in the Gospel of John.

Also contained within the New Testament are the writings of Paul. These writings have had an incredible impact of much of the history and thinking to be found in Christianity's over two thousand year life! In addition, the Bible's concluding book, the Book of Revelation, is well known as a book which delves into all kinds of varied interpretations, for sure, many of which simply do NOT reflect the original intents and purposes of the book.

The Book of Revelation has been used as the foundation of many books and movies, such as the Left Behind series. Most theologians and denominations do not think that the kind of "end times" scenarios which the authors and producers of those construct are justified by scripture. Within two hundred years of the writing of the book, a noted theologian remarked that Revelation was a very symbolic book, and the key to the symbolism had been lost.

But many people have since enjoyed trying to reconstruct that symbolism!

THE BIG ISSUE

What is important to realize as you read about Jesus is this: it is difficult not to find that many of his earliest followers expected that He would return soon and bring peace upon the earth, fulfilling the Messianic hopes and dreams of his fellow Jewish people.

Here is the thing:

He did not return physically to this earth. There was no 'messianic age.' And, in those over two thousand years since, HE HAS

NOT RETURNED. In that time, generations have come and gone.

The Result

Over the course of the history that has unfolded since that time, the community of Jesus' followers known as 'the church' has developed different interpretations of what Jesus taught. They have developed teachings, known also as doctrines, to both sum up and explain the meaning of Jesus' life and death and their faith in his resurrection. Within Christianity, there are different interpretations. These different interpretations of what Jesus taught and what He expects of his church has, over the course of time, led to a wide variety of different 'churches.'

What I am saying is that I am assuming that if you were to take a twenty mile drive and go through several different neighborhoods not far from where you live, you might very well pass by a lot of different churches. By the way, this is a great activity. I have had lots of classes of adolescents I have taught do it!!! The reason there are so many is that over the course of time, different people have looked at Jesus and emphasized certain points that have eventually found their way into doctrine and also church policy and laws.

What all of these churches have in common is a belief in the importance of Jesus and his message but they also might very well differ on how to interpret that message. Many people find this frustrating and confusing. My point to you is simply that this is a basic reality and my encouragement to you is to keep on seeking ways to learn as much as you possibly can about Jesus—his background, the influences upon him and what he really taught.

I encourage you also to reflect upon him and ask yourself what influence he might possibly be in your life. It is a question to which we will return later on in this book but for now we need to take a brief look at some other significant religious approaches that exist in our world today, along the way making points of comparison with Christianity. This is not intended to be a thorough overview of any of these approaches, just a simple starting point for your future research and a way of placing Christianity in broader context. As a matter of fact, one could argue that I have left some important traditions out. As this is not a 'world religions' textbook, I encourage you to research both these and other traditions (Taoism and Confucianism come to mind). I present these great traditions as important starting points for your deeper exploration of this topic:

HINDUISM - The oldest living religion in the world, emerging out of India. It emphasizes a system of many incarnations of the divine, all in relationship to the divine in the universe. It sees each soul as on a journey to reach 'Nirvana' and souls traveling into other bodies in the course of its lifetime, a view known as 'reincarnation.'

BUDDHISM - Evolved from Hinduism with emphasis on 'right thinking and action' grounded in meditation. Less focus on a deity as such (and for some Buddhists, an atheistic religion). It has been a source of influence over time for such movements as Transcendental Meditation and mindfulness.

JUDAISM - The religious approach of Jesus, which places emphasis on the Law and the Prophets. There are different branches within Judaism with some expecting a Messiah to return and others awaiting the coming of a "Messianic Age' where peace and justice shall reign at last.

ISLAM - Recognizes the prophet Muhammad as the latest and ultimate revelation from God. Also recognizes the importance of the prophets, including Jesus.

CONCLUSION

My suggestion to you, as you consider Christian faith, is also to be attuned to points of connection between Christianity and other religious approaches. In other words, I encourage you to look for areas in which the teachings of Jesus and the basic spiritual impulses that are part of being human are found in the expressions of the different religious approaches. What I am saying is that one can be an avowed Christian and learn from, pray with and join hands in unity with Jews, Muslims, Buddhists, Hindus and those of other 'religious' traditions.

I will take it a step further and contend that one can call one-self a 'follower of Jesus' and gladly work with those who say they are atheists and agnostics in seeking such goals as world peace and social justice. In a world so painfully divided, we need to find these points of connection.

Being a believing Christian should help attain the goal of human unity. It should never be an obstacle. It should never stand in its way!

QUESTIONS FOR DISCUSSION

1. What is your belief about Jesus?
2. If you could ask Jesus a couple of questions, what would you ask?
3. As a class project, consider going by all of the churches within a ten mile radius of where you live. List the different church names and do research about the denominations or larger church communities of which they are a part (ex: Roman Catholic, Lutheran, Episcopal, etc). Discuss your findings with your class if you are a part of one.
4. Using information available from a reliable online resource (Wikipedia is acceptable), research a religion which is not Christian in detail. If part of a group, report your findings and give your opinions about it, specifying how it deals with issues of ORIGIN, DESTINY, and MEANING.

CHAPTER FIVE

THE GOD QUESTION

In the last chapter, we took a look at Jesus. While individuals may differ on some specifics, most Christians would acknowledge that we turn to Jesus to get a glimpse of God. Certainly the early followers of Jesus saw in his life, death, and resurrection, the expression of who God is and what God is all about. In fact, when you look at different DOCTRINES (beliefs) that Christians hold, the one representing a conviction concerning THE INCARNATION is about as high on the list as they come.

What that means exactly could be subject for considerable discussion, wouldn't you say?

> **The Doctrine of the Incarnation is the concept that, in Jesus, God became human.**

So, certainly, the God question is a significant one in exploring the life of Jesus. Yet, whether an individual is a Christian believer, an atheist or comes from a different perspective than either, any look at God requires a serious exploration of what any of us mean when we talk about God. Were I to say to you right now that even people who believe in God tend to share similar beliefs, I really would not be very accurate.

Below you will find listed several questions about God. These are questions that are intended to get you thinking about what you think about when you see or hear the word God. They also might provide you some insight regarding the considerable variety of 'God beliefs and definitions' that exist in our world. These variations exist within the framework of existing religions. In other words, one could be a Christian and really hold to a different way of looking at God from someone who shares a similar faith. Now, some people would be very frightened by this. I am not — and I will tell you why.

It is my conviction that when we are talking about God, we are in an area of great mystery. As a Biblical writer has said "No one has ever seen God." We place faith that there is a God but honestly are short on a few specifics. Have you ever seen the movie *Rudy*? In it, a kind elderly Catholic priest says to the young man, Rudy, "In all my years of experience, I have learned two things: There is a God and I am not Him." Actually, I would add that calling God 'Him' does not tell the whole story either.

To be a human being is to recognize that we are limited. We are NOT the source of life. We don't know all the answers. An honest reading of the Bible shows numerous passages where people of faith recognize that they just don't have the whole picture. In a great section which you should read, I Corinthians 13, the author, Paul, writes: 'Now I see dimly, as in a mirror...' A phenomenal religious writer by the name of Paul Tillich who wrote thousands of words about God summed much of his work up by simply saying 'GOD is a name for God!'

So what I am saying to you is that you can be deeply spiritual or religious or whatever term you want to use to connote the fact that your life is connected to a power greater than yourself and still say with honest conviction that you don't know all the answers and that your attempt to define God carries within it some strong degree of inaccuracy because ... you are not God!

Now, to be honest, there are those in the Christian community who would argue against my perspective. They are oftentimes defined as Fundamentalists or as part of Evangelical Christianity, though, in some ways, that is a terrible misuse of the word evangelical. Evangelical is really a good word, linked to the concept of spreading the 'good news' that Jesus brings. Yet many these days who call themselves 'evangelical' would identify as 'conservative, Bible believing Christians,' and many among them follow interpretations of the Bible which provide unfortunate justification for discrimination and denial of human rights. Sadly, that description has pretty much taken over the word 'evangelical.' Too bad! Anyway, their perspective is different from mine — and you should know it.

Here is what these 'conservative, Bible believing' Christians would argue:

1. The Bible is the **infallible** Word of God. That means in it, we find God's truth.
2. If you want to know who God is and what God thinks, it is all there in the Bible.
3. The Bible describes an all powerful and all knowing God. Though there are differences even among conservative Christians, many hold to the claim that God both knows all things before they happen and that what happens is part of His sovereign will. I need to be clear: There ARE variations on this idea among conservative Christians.
4. The Bible shows that God sent His only Son Jesus who by His death bought our salvation.
5. The Bible makes clear that the one way to salvation is found in Jesus.

To make clear, this is what I am not saying:

1. I am not saying that the Bible cannot be described as the Word of God. What I **am** saying is that what the Bible teaches is not always completely clear. In fact, there **are** Biblical passages

that do contradict other Bible passages. *As example, please compare comments on 'an eye for an eye, a tooth for a tooth' found in Exodus, Deuteronomy or Leviticus with what Jesus says as recorded in the Gospel of Matthew. You can do this by simply 'googling' this phrase and placing the Biblical book title near it.*

2. I am not saying that the Bible does not give a glimpse of God. I **am** saying that it is written through the experiences of human beings who do not have all the answers and, in addition, it gives a whole lot of glimpses as to how different people see God — with their own different points of emphasis drawn, I would suggest, from, among other things, their own personal experiences.

3. I am not saying that various passages of the Bible do not describe an all powerful, all knowing God. I am saying that others show a different picture — of a God who has been victimized and whose power is found in weakness. Let's look at Jesus on the Cross! Or take a read of the Book of Job, a Biblical book I suggest you explore sometime in depth. When you read it, please read it along with Rabbi Harold Kushner's *When Bad Things Happen to Good People.*

4. I am not saying that the Bible does not make the case that Jesus is the way to salvation. I am saying that the Christian Bible was written in a particular geographic area at a particularly specific point in history — and that God's salvation extends far beyond that because **God** extends beyond geography and era in time!

I put all of this out there before you read further because I want you to know that there will be those within the Christian community who will really quarrel with much of what I am writing. What I am asking you to do is to really get in touch with how you are receiving this material. If you are reading this as part of a class, please get involved in asking questions and in challenging what I write if any of it strikes you as not making sense.

What you will read below is an attempt to show the different ways in which GOD is understood and expressed in language. Please realize that even when I make generalizations about certain believers holding some beliefs in common, even among those who share a set of beliefs, there are differences in understanding and interpretation among them. Printed below is an ancient statement of faith professed in many churches on Sundays. It is called the Nicene Creed and it reached its current form in the 4th century. I am fine with saying in the 4th century.

Now, we say this Creed or a shorter one called The Apostles Creed in my church every Sunday of the year. Oftentimes, as I have been saying it, I have at same time wondered as to what these words mean to those worshiping with me who are saying them also. What I mean is that each person hears and says these words and interprets them through the filters of her/his own life experience, what she/he has been taught and even the questions and concerns that person might be facing in her/his life at that particular moment. Certain phrases may stand out for affirmation or questioning depending on how you are experiencing life in the here and now.

So, take a look at these words — and then read them slowly. Think about what is going on inside of you as you read them or speak them. What stands out? Makes no sense? Pushes you in the direction of asking questions? Makes you want to simply say' Yes, I believe that!'? OK, ready? Here goes:

> We believe in one God,
>   the Father, the Almighty,
>   maker of heaven and earth,
>   of all that is, seen and unseen.
> We believe in one Lord, Jesus Christ,
>   the only Son of God,
>   eternally begotten of the Father,
>   God from God, Light from Light,
>   true God from true God,
>   begotten, not made,

of one Being with the Father.
Through him all things were made.
For us and for our salvation
   he came down from heaven:
by the power of the Holy Spirit
   he became incarnate from the Virgin Mary,
   and was made man.
For our sake he was crucified under Pontius Pilate;
   he suffered death and was buried.
   On the third day he rose again
      in accordance with the Scriptures;
   he ascended into heaven
      and is seated at the right hand of the Father.
He will come again in glory to judge the living and the dead,
   and his kingdom will have no end.
We believe in the Holy Spirit, the Lord, the giver of life,
   who proceeds from the Father and the Son.
With the Father and the Son he is worshiped and glorified.
He has spoken through the Prophets.
We believe in one holy catholic and apostolic Church.
We acknowledge one baptism for the forgiveness of sins.
We look for the resurrection of the dead,
   and the life of the world to come. Amen.

(This creed is regularly spoken in Catholic, Episcopal and Lutheran churches as part of Sunday worship).

Wow! There is a lot there, wouldn't you say? Depending upon which Christian church with which you are affiliated, how you are taught this Creed will be dealt with differently. Some Christians will say that this Creed represents the clear, true faith of the church and that believing in it is essential for calling oneself a member of that church. Other Christians see it as one among many important statements of faith that have developed over the course of religious history. You won't see it recited very often in their churches, if at all! Still others recognize in it a kind of poetic language which attempts to express a great mystery but also recognize that you can't completely capture the mystery that is God in words.

Now, when I read and profess (and I do profess) this Creed, I also have to say that I find the word 'Father' to be somewhat limited. You see, 'father' is a human term, from human experience, for God and while it does make sense to call God 'father,' one could readily, in my view, describe God as 'mother' too. Now fundamentalists would have a problem with this because they would say that 'The Bible says that God is father.' Yet we also realize that if you study the Bible, you will also find a lot of female language for God. A lot has been written about this topic by those who study the Bible.

Now, here is the thing: The Nicene Creed was written by men! I am talking about people of the male gender! As a result, living in a male dominated culture, they tended to use language that emphasized the male. Think about it. Even today, unfortunately, in my view, a lot of people regularly say 'mankind' when they are describing humanity or they say 'brothers' in church readings when they mean brothers and sisters. Most modern Americans believe men and women are created equal, yet we use language saying 'all men are.'

So, what I am saying is that when I say the Creed, while I agree that God is like a father, I also think mother imagery describes God too. So, therefore, I can profess God as father, mother and, as the Bible shows many other descriptive names as well — names like wind, spirit, rock and so on....

You see, what I am contending is that human language, in attempting to describe God, is actually describing the indescribable. Likewise, it is an attempt to explain the unexplainable. So, therefore, I think we need to use what I would call expansive language to describe 'the divine,' that which we call by the name of God. Expansive language broadens the terminology we use to describe God. As I see it, it is more accurate simply because it is not limiting. God is greater than any individual name we can give 'her or him,' i.e. any individual name we can give the presence of the divine

that we call 'God.' This is precisely the reason why some religious
expressions don't even speak or write the name 'God.' I freely do
because I think the name speaks to profound meaning and reality,
but I appreciate the insight given by those who do not.

Now, of course, we are human beings so we relate to the personal. We communicate with each other as persons. Therefore, in
thinking about relating to God we readily turn to personal language
— describing God as father, friend, and so much more — and,
generally speaking, taking our experience of relating to human
beings and projecting those qualities on God.

That is not a bad thing so long as we understand that we are
doing it and that we recognize that we don't can't fully describe or
comprehend God. Sadly, many Christians really feel that they know
exactly why things happen and what God is thinking in making
them happen.

At this point, as I said above, I would like to suggest that you
take some time and read the first 39 chapters of the Book of Job.
The basic bottom line of Job is that you have this guy who is a really
good person and, for no apparent reason, bad things start to happen
to him. He then wonders why God is making them happen.

What is great about this book — and if you are in class with
a teacher who is willing to do this — is that it is the perfect book
in the Bible to help promote a lively discussion....

In reading Job, I suggest you ask these questions:

Does God determine what happens to us?
Does God make good and bad things happen?
How does God support us when bad things happen to us?
Does God support us when bad things happen?

You might even want to talk about this powerful prayer:

We cannot merely pray to You, O God, to end war;
For we know that You have made the world in a way
So that all of us must find our own path to peace,
Within ourselves and with our neighbors.

We cannot merely pray to You, O God, to end hunger;
For you have already given us the resources
With which to feed the entire world,
If we would only use them wisely.

We cannot merely pray to You, O God,
    to root out our prejudice;
For You have already given us eyes
With which to see the good in all people,
If we would only use them rightly.

We cannot merely pray to you, O God, to end despair;
For You have already given us the power
To clear away slums and to give hope,
If we would only use our power justly.

We cannot merely pray to You, O God, to end disease;
For You have already given us great minds
With which to search out cures and healing,
If we could only use them constructively.

Therefore, we pray to You instead, O God,
For strength, determination, and courage,
To do instead of just to pray,
To become instead of merely to wish.

This is a prayer I first found in an amazing book to which I referred above, (*When Bad Things Happen to Good People* by Rabbi Harold Kushner.) In it, Kushner tries to deal with an awful tragedy in his life by attempting to figure out the place that God plays in it. It is a book that, however you feel about this wonderful rabbi's conclusions, is bound to get you thinking about how YOU view God....

Now, back to the Nicene Creed.

You see, if you look at that Creed, you will find in it an attempt by Christians in the 4th century to do their very best to state what is so important about this Jesus in whom they had come to believe. Among other things, it is an attempt to deal with the question of Jesus and how he fits into the big picture of God.

The statement of faith that IS this Creed centers around this:

Christians believe that if you take a look at Jesus, you are taking a look at the presence of God among us. The technical phrase is that Christians believe that God is incarnate, that is, was fully human and experienced life as human, in a human body — in Jesus.

This gets a bit complicated, however, because this conviction is centered on the idea that Jesus never stops being fully human. The essence of the Incarnation is that Jesus IS human. A lot of Christians over the years have emphasized Jesus' 'divine powers,' e.g. turning water into wine. They have basically said 'Well, OK, he is human, but here is proof that he is God too.'

It is not as simple as that:

Stories about miracle workers were pretty common around Jesus' time, as I mentioned before. Jesus was not alone in having people say he could do miraculous things.

The Bible is a literary work and certain things are going to be written to highlight the deeper truth beneath the story with a recognition that truth is broader and deeper than 'factual truth.'

What I am really saying to you, the reader, is that I want you and your classmates or friends to think about this and to talk about these questions:

What do you think of when you think of God?

Is God present in your life? How? How do you know that?

Is God alive? How? How do you know that?

Could God eliminate evil from the earth? If yes, why does God not do so? (Notice — I didn't say "Why doesn't HE?".)

Do you believe Jesus is God? Explain.

What language and terminology best expresses for YOU the reality of GOD?

Let's go deeper ...

With which of the following do you agree and why?

God created the world and knows everything that is happening right now.

God is a strong spiritual force but does not really know things the way we understand humans to know stuff.

God set the world in motion and is uninvolved.

God has predetermined everything that is going to happen.

I believe deeply in God, but can't pretend to tell you that I know all of the answers about how God functions — and that's OK!

As a human being, I can't know anything about God.

As a human being, I can't know as much about God as I tend to think I know.

When I see Jesus, I see God. If this is your position, please explain!

As a matter of fact, wouldn't it be great to write a 500-word statement describing your belief about God and then share it in a discussion with your peers? By the way, feel free to email me this statement or post it on my blog!

BEFORE WE FINISH THIS CHAPTER

Part of what I am doing here is to try to get you to think and to process your thoughts in the presence of others if at all possible. It is based on my premise that when we talk about God, we are talking about mystery. Yet, as an individual who calls himself a Christian and as a pastor responsible for leading congregations in trying to live out Christian faith, it is also important that I make my own position clear on this subject, the subject of God. The problem is in how I do this without closing the door on your own inquiry and the process of your asking deep and profound questions.

I want to strike a balance. I want to clue you in on what I believe while encouraging you to continue to reflect on where you are RIGHT NOW and in all of the right now's that lie ahead. If you are part of a group reading this book, I hope you engage in great discussion. If you are not, try to find ways to discuss these questions I have raised and which you have read.

Allow me to explain for you where I stand: Ever since I was very young, I have 'believed in God.' I continue to do so. In fact, 'belief in God' constitutes the core and essence of my own existence. Yet, this belief in God has gone through periods of growth and change, times in which I described God in different terms than I might now or in which I went through life unaware that there were certain ways to understand and reflect upon God. So, at times I emphasized in my own thinking and teaching certain things I had come to believe about God.

As I live in my sixties (age, not decade. I have already been through the decade!), I am very comfortable saying this: I believe in God. I believe there IS a love that permeates the universe, a love poured out into creation. I believe that this God continues to be present in creation, that this God is expressed and incarnate in the human being Jesus of Nazareth. I believe that this Jesus, though once crucified, continues to live. I very freely and gladly affirm my faith in a God described in the ancient language of Father, Son, and Spirit, even as I contend that some of the language has to be expanded! I love reading different peoples' reflections about the meaning behind certain teachings. The more reading I do, the deeper I find myself immersed in the mystery of God which underlines for me the importance of God in my life.

Now, were I you, I would ask: how do you know that? And, to you I would say that is a fair question: Make me probe it, encourage me to question it…This much I can say, though- the more I have been pushed by questions and doubts, the more have I found that which I have believed all along, however much how I express it is so different from what I may have said at 8 or 10 or 12 or 30…. I believe it ever more deeply every day I live my life….

As this chapter draws to its end, I am left with two different quotes.

Of myself, the words of Bob Dylan always seem to speak for me as indeed they do here:

'I was so much older then. I'm younger than that now.'

These words carry within me that which youth celebrates — a willingness to question, to discard that which makes no sense and to integrate into oneself a variety of experiences and perspective, all possible because of one's willingness to be open to life ... and to learn ...

For you, I offer you again that quote from Rainer Maria Rilke I expressed earlier that inspired me so much when I was so much younger (or was it older?):

'Be patient toward all that is unsolved in your heart and try to love the questions themselves.'

Hope you have some great conversations!! Ideas for conversations are found within this chapter!

CHAPTER SIX

AN HONEST LOOK AT PRAYER:

WHAT IT IS AND IS NOT

When people think about religion, one of the things with which they usually associate it with is the practice of prayer. I begin this chapter by asking you to consider the simple question: Why do you think people pray? I would get more personal and ask another: Do you pray and if you do, what do you think happens in and through your act of prayer?

As you consider this, here are some things I want you to think about. I am listing here some common reasons why people pray:

On some level, they feel that prayer can change the outcome. Maybe it can change God's mind. This, of course, is all connected to our notion of how we view God — is God active in our lives? Involved? Capable of stepping in? Or has God wound up the world and are we all running on our own?

Some people don't know what else to do, so they simply pray. Maybe it's part of their religious tradition. Perhaps they are operating on the level of superstition. Maybe they just don't know.

Others might tell others I am praying for you and do, but are completely unsure if it would have any impact. Yet, there is goodness in their saying is because it is a way of saying that they care.

Prayer, of course, is all over the Bible — and I would contend that these different approaches to prayer are all over it as well. You have people bargaining with God, pouring out their emotion, or simply praying that they do 'God's Will.' Now, for what it is worth, I would like to contribute to your discussion by offering some of my thoughts:

I believe that prayer is ultimately INTENTIONALLY PLACING OURSELVES IN THE PRESENCE OF GOD, WHO IS BOTH LOVE AND MYSTERY. In other words, at its core, prayer is an honest human recognition that 'I am NOT God.' I would suggest that in that presence and before that presence, we can lay out our thoughts, fears, hopes, dreams, stupid things we have done, preferences for our future...

We can tell God what we are hoping for other people as well, believing down deep inside that God loves all of the people I love with an incredible depth.

Yet, we do all of this understanding that:

We are not doing it superstitiously

We are not doing it to pile up points or make God do it the way we want

Instead, our prayer becomes our recognition that, as human beings, we live much of our lives enshrouded in mystery. We don't REALLY know what lies ahead. We don't know the actual causation of much of what will happen, i.e. how much is human decision, how much is God, nor do we really know the what's and how's of God's own 'will'....

BUT WE PRAY ... We pray to acknowledge that there is more than what we see within this universe. In fact, we pray because much of what we see may very well express something far deeper than all that we see.

To all of you reading this and discussing this, I have a couple of other questions for you as well: If you say to someone 'I will pray for you', what do you really mean? Are you saying this as a way to say that you care? Maybe if that's what you are saying, why not just say you care? OR ... are you saying that whatever that person is going through, you are going to bring it into your conscious relationship with God, even though, being human, you don't really have a handle on cause and effect?

Yet, you see, you don't have to have such a handle. It is enough to bring it to God because if you do, you are connecting with a presence far more powerful than you, yet a presence that somehow lives within.

My other question is this: Where is praying with other people in your life? How important to you is it to pray as part of a group and using the words and music that you would use in a service in a church? This whole question of 'prayer in common' is one worthy of significant conversation!

The bottom line in all of this is pretty straightforward, in my view: Make of your life a prayer. In Paul's words, pray always, but pray sincerely and humbly... and do not make of prayer a superstition!!

QUESTIONS FOR THOUGHT AND DISCUSSION

1. What is the difference between prayer and superstition?
2. Do you think prayer is important? Why or why not?
3. If you pray, how do you pray? How important to you is praying with other people, as in praying 'in church'?
4. How does the prayer style of your church help or hinder your life of prayer?

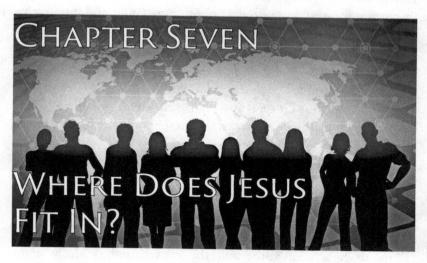

CHAPTER SEVEN

WHERE DOES JESUS FIT IN?

s I have tried to say throughout this little book, my strongest suggestion to you is that you try your best to learn about Jesus. In order to do so, my suggestion is that you concentrate on these two things:

The stories he told

The way he treated others

Now, in doing that, I am likewise suggesting that, at this point, you pay less attention to:

What the church teaches about Jesus

The supernatural, miraculous nature of some of what is written in the Bible about Jesus.

This is not intended to downplay any parts of the Bible-or to disrespect the importance of the church. While I am sure some would disagree with my suggestions to you, here is what I am trying to say: I don't want you to be so caught up in what people are saying ABOUT JESUS or about Jesus' 'supernatural powers' that what gets lost in the process is WHAT HE TAUGHT and HOW HE LIVED HIS LIFE.

Personally, in my view, the miraculous stuff is important in unraveling much of the faith that has been part of the life of

Christianity. In addition, the teachings of particular churches are important for us to know, reflect upon, pray about and if reflective of our own faith, to put into practice and expression. Yet, what I am saying is that we do not want to lose the power of what he said and did.

So, to this end, I encourage that you do this:

Go to the four Gospels and read every single parable of Jesus. If you had to prioritize, start with Luke 15 and the three parables of the lost coin, lost sheep and lost (prodigal) son.

Read Chapters 5 through 7 in the Gospel of Matthew, as I have mentioned before. Fast forward then to Matthew 25.

Read the accounts of Jesus as he faced His own crucifixion and how he refused to use violence when his life was threatened.

Read the parables of the Good Samaritan, the story of Jesus talking to the woman at the well, the one where the sinful woman washes his feet, yet another where he saves a woman caught in adultery from being stoned to death. Go on to his conversations on the Cross and, of course, his prayer in the Garden of Gethsemane.

Look to what he pointed out as the greatest commandment and why and run through all four gospels and get a feel for his general attitude toward those society might see as 'outcasts.'

From all of that material, talk with others about the following:

What was most important to Jesus?

What was his view of God?

What was his understanding of 'unconditional love'?

How important was forgiveness to him?

What did he think about violence and using force?

What was his view of women?

What was his understanding of the purpose of religion?

Was Jesus in any way radical?

Why do you think Jesus would be such an inspiration for people like Martin Luther King or Mahatma Gandhi?

Why was he such a threat to those in power?

Now, this is a short chapter, but there is an awful lot of material here, both for thought and discussion. To be honest, my big concern is that in this world of Christian religion, we can get so caught up in the world of the rules and policies and teachings of different Christian religions that we lose sight of how incredible a teacher Jesus really was. I hope that this chapter and the discussion you will have about the questions I ask within it is of real value to you as you encounter this incredible man!

As an exercise, it would be valuable to read about Martin Luther King and also Dorothy Day, Oscar Romero and Dietrich Bonhoeffer, as well as Pope Francis in our own day, all of whom were deeply influenced in various ways by Jesus. Why were they so influenced?

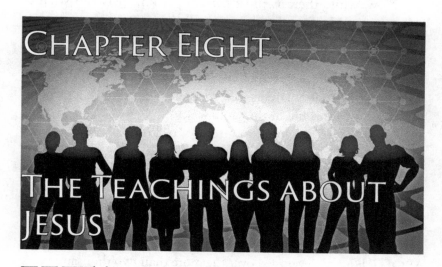

CHAPTER EIGHT

THE TEACHINGS ABOUT JESUS

While it is a historical fact that a man named Jesus of Nazareth existed, the development of a faith called CHRISTIANITY was based on what people believed about him! This is where we see some significant differences among religious points of view. MANY people who acknowledge the worth and value of what Jesus taught do NOT call themselves Christians because there are certain claims they will not make about him. For example, Mahatma Gandhi admired Jesus greatly, but identified himself as a Hindu, not a Christian. He is not alone!

If you have been part of a church or are considering the possibility of joining one, you have most likely been exposed to many teachings about Jesus. These are beliefs about WHO HE IS and the meaning of his life that are part of the life of your church. If you are part of a church that professes or teaches the value of such historic creeds as the Nicene and Apostles Creed we mentioned in previous chapters, you have been exposed to many teachings about Jesus. Oftentimes, you will hear people say that they admire Jesus but struggle with the concept of 'church' because they feel organized religion has other emphases than Jesus did in his own life.

Now, while there is most certainly a link between what is believed about Jesus and who Jesus really is, we also have to understand that the beliefs represent interpretations about the meaning of his life. Not all interpretations are held by all people who admire Jesus or who 'believe in Him'. Likewise, people can basically agree on a lot of facts about Jesus' life without necessarily interpreting the meaning of his life in the same way.

So, what we are going to attempt to do here is to construct three categories for your consideration. The first category will contain some facts about the life of Jesus, generally acknowledged to be accurate whether people believe IN Jesus or not. These are some established facts about the man Jesus of Nazareth and his followers. The second category will state some facts that happened AFTER his death. The third category will include some established teachings ABOUT Jesus as developed over the more than two thousand years that the church, the community of Christian believers, has existed. After we get through these lists, we will talk about the significance in the difference between the facts and the beliefs.

FACTS ABOUT JESUS

(Some of these are referred to in a previous chapter. They are repeated here so that you can contrast them with the emergence of teachings ABOUT Him)

He grew up in Nazareth and his mother was Mary.

He was raised as part of the Jewish religious tradition.

At around the age of thirty, He found the direction of his life and began traveling throughout the region in the Middle East known today as Israel.

In his travels, he told stories known as parables, was recognized as healing some folks, and associated with individuals who were highly criticized by the religious establishment of his day.

He bothered a lot of religious leaders. They saw him as 'soft on religious laws' inclined to include in his group of followers those generally acknowledged as public sinners.

His message contained powerful lessons focusing in on the universal love of God and God's forgiving nature.

He was seen as a threat to the established religious and political order.

For his crimes, he was sentenced to death.

On the night before he died, he shared a meal with his closest friends, identifying the broken bread and wine poured out as indicative of the death he was about to face.

He was crucified and died.

FACTS ABOUT WHAT HAPPENED AFTER JESUS DIED

Jesus was buried in a tomb.

While there are some differences in the specifics of the story, word began to spread among some of his closest friends (disciples/followers) that he was not dead, but was alive.

Several people reported personal experiences of encountering this risen Jesus.

While the evidence shows that he did not remain physically upon the earth, those closest to him understood that their mission was to get the word out about him as they anticipated the day when his reign would be established, most likely upon the earth.

The community we now know as the 'church' emerged as a result of the belief of these early disciples of Jesus that Jesus indeed was the fulfillment of the promises of their faith.

Jesus did not return to earth.

These new followers underwent various persecutions.

This new Christian faith spread beyond its original geographic location.

What began as a community of disciples in an isolated geographic region became a collection of communities separated by distance.

Eventually, this religious movement called 'Christianity' became the established religion of the Roman Empire.

Now, if you are reading this and have been raised within a church, you might be thinking: 'Wait a minute, you have left a lot out here!' If you are thinking that, you are right! What I have left out is what you are about to read in this next category. In it, we will look at the BELIEFS that have developed about this Jesus. Some scholars have referred to this as the difference between the 'Christ of faith' and the 'Jesus of history'. What you should also know as well is that as churches developed, some churches also began to emphasize certain beliefs about Jesus more than some other churches do. What I would suggest is that in looking at this list, you talk in your class or group (or with some others) about how you interpret the importance of what has been taught about Jesus.

BELIEFS ABOUT JESUS WHICH DEVELOPED OVER TIME

Jesus is 'the Christ.' You see, CHRIST is a title meaning 'anointed one' or 'Messiah.' It was not Jesus' last name. To call Jesus 'Christ' is a statement of faith.

Jesus was raised from the dead.

Jesus returned to (ascended into) heaven.

Jesus established a community of disciples (church) that would spread his message and celebrate sacraments in His name.

Jesus was, in the words of the Nicene Creed. 'God from God, Light from Light, true God from true God.'

The birth of Jesus was a 'virgin birth.'

Jesus was to be understood as a 'personal Savior.'

Accepting Christ as Savior was important in terms of personal 'salvation.'

Because of Jesus, eternal happiness in God's presence is made possible.

Jesus will come again.

THREE IMPORTANT NOTES

Over the course of time, as the institution known as the 'church' grew, it became clear that Christians had differences of opinion among themselves. The most obvious example of this was the historical movement known as the 'Reformation' in the 16th century. Prior to that, there was the 'Great Schism' in 1054 which led to the separation of the Roman Catholic and Orthodox churches. The bottom line with both of those movements is that it is very clear that not all Christians view what we call Christian belief (doctrine) in the same way. There are differences. If YOU are part of a church community, you HAVE learned and will be learning about the long-standing tradition of your church/denomination on the topics I have listed above. Likewise, different churches have different views regarding how important it is to accept specific church teachings in order to be part of that church community. I hope you have the opportunity to explore and discuss this. If you are not part of a church community, please look for local opportunities to explore Christian churches, perhaps attending classes and/ or meeting with pastors for conversation, something I did 'when I was your age'!

One of the biggest areas of difference has to do with how one sees the Bible. Many established beliefs of many Christians are based on their interpretation that 'The Bible teaches this.' This literal, fundamentalist view of the Bible which we talked about earlier makes some interpretations threatening to people not from that perspective. Other Christians see the Bible as more complex and not always quite as clear as the way Fundamentalists see it.

For many Christians, most notably those in the Roman Catholic tradition, the role of the teaching authority of the church takes on a great significance in determining what to believe. Catholic teaching emphasizes that Jesus gave teaching authority to his church in the way he established the role of Peter. Catholics see the Bishop of Rome (Pope) as successor of Peter. Now, to be fair, you will find many Catholics who will disagree among themselves as to the extent and scope of the authority of the Pope. Nonetheless, this view that there is teaching authority within the church is a significant constitutive element of Catholicism. What is interesting, however, is that many Fundamentalist churches, even without a Pope, place a lot of teaching authority in the hands of individual pastors or teachers too!

WHERE DO CHRISTIANS AGREE?

With all of this variation, what are the points of agreement between and among those of us who call ourselves Christians? In constructing this list, I am well aware that some might say it does not include enough. What I would like you to do is to think and talk about both what you think of what is on the list and what you might add as important to you. Having said that, here goes:

God exists and is alive and active.

God is uniquely present in Jesus.

Jesus is alive and present in the world and the acts of 'the church,' which have traditionally been called 'sacraments.'

The church is a community initiated by Jesus, a community which affirms that 'Christ has died, Christ is Risen, Christ will come again,' though differing on how some of that either happened or may take place.

Believing in Jesus requires that beliefs be put into action and that it is important to try to live our lives based on the values and teachings of Jesus.

If you are reading this book and are part of a group or class at a particular Christian church, I encourage you to explore in depth how your church approaches questions about Jesus. Learn as much as you can about the background which has led to some of the formulations of your church. Wherever possible, explore the different ways in which Jesus has been viewed historically. Explore the lives of people who have been strongly influenced by Jesus, trying your best to become aware of people from different perspectives and life situations. If you are reading this on your own, I suggest you consider exploring some of this reading material and finding someone to have conversations with about the topics therein.

Regardless of where you may find yourself standing on some particular questions of church teaching, I hope you are excited about the message Jesus brought, the person Jesus is and the presence He continues to be in our world today.

DISCUSSION QUESTIONS

1. Which of the above beliefs about Jesus do you find most important to you?
2. With which beliefs do you most struggle?
3. Look up some hymns about Jesus in your church hymnal or a Christian hymnal you research. Look for ways in which Jesus is described. Discuss some hymns that express what YOU believe about Jesus. If applicable, discuss some hymns that contain ideas with which you struggle.
4. How would you answer the question of Jesus: 'Who do YOU say that I am?'

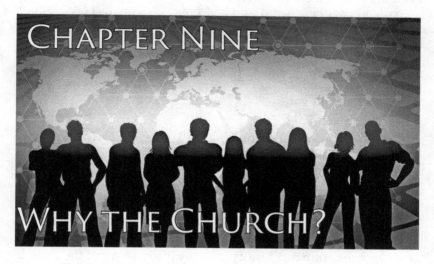

IS CHRISTIANITY POSSIBLE WITHOUT THE CHURCH?

Drive through the streets of the cities and towns that constitute the landscape of both your country and others and you will find an awful lot of buildings called churches. For most people, when they think of church they think of these kinds of buildings. At the same time, there are groups of people who worship in peoples' homes who also call the group of people with whom they gather and worship a 'church' as well. Technically speaking, a church consists of people. Historically, organized groups of people who call themselves church have constructed a lot of buildings that go by the name 'church,' but the reality is that, technically speaking, the church IS people.

You see, the Christian church consists of people who seek to 'follow' Jesus. While it is acceptable to say 'I am going to church on Sunday morning,' it is also acceptable, and even more accurate to say 'I am part of a church community that is going to this building on Park Avenue to gather with other followers of Jesus for worship.' So, at core, the church is people, people who take seriously and seek to be disciples of Jesus. There is accuracy in the old churchy joke…

> 'How do you spell CHURCH?'
> Answer: 'CH__CH'
> Response: What's missing? YOU (U) ARE (R)!

OK, the joke is corny but the point is clear: THE CHURCH IS PEOPLE, and they, the people who comprise the church, (we) pay attention to what Jesus said and try to follow His directives. They (We) do this because of what we believe about Him.

Over the course of history, this institution we call the church has grown and is associated by many with two major activities:

Building and maintaining church buildings and oftentimes institutions sponsored by that church, e.g. schools, hospitals, orphanages…

Holding to and teaching certain BELIEFS — about Jesus and about what we as followers of Jesus should do.

One of the great dividing points in the history of the church stems from what is considered by many to be a very important belief. Roman Catholics believe that the person called Pope is the leader of the church and acts in the modern world as they understand Peter acted in the early days of the church, in those years after Jesus walked the face of this earth. Those who call themselves Protestants see it differently. They do not believe that this is the kind of earthly authority that Jesus commanded.

Fortunately, over the last few decades, there has been a greater emphasis among many Christian churches on what Christians believe in common and less on what sets us apart from each other. Nonetheless, the fact remains that the way in which certain groups of believers, including organized churches, view different issues highlights the fact that you and someone else can both call yourselves Christians, yet you may hold significantly different beliefs on topics such as gay marriage, divorce and remarriage, the use of alcohol, the rights of immigrants, gun control and what constitutes a just war. Many organized larger church groups have significant differences with each other over a variety of issues.

Having said this, I hope you find it helpful if I break down the place of organized Christian churches in the following way:

Both Roman Catholicism and Orthodoxy trace their roots to the beginnings of the Christian movement. Roman Catholicism holds to the claim that the Pope holds an unique position of authority in church teaching and trace the origins of the Pope's authority to Jesus' declaration to Peter that Peter was the rock upon which He (Jesus) would build His church.

The Protestant Reformation in the 16th century led to the breaking away of many European based churches from the Catholic Church in the 16th century. The great Reformers challenged the Roman Catholic interpretation of authority in the church, in particular the claims Catholicism made regarding the Papacy.

If you ever have been affiliated with an organized 'church' or even with a more loosely affiliated church community or home church, how you got to where you are is traceable back to these possibilities.

With that in mind, I encourage you to delve into the history of your church affiliation, if you have one, discovering answers to these questions:

What are this church's core beliefs — about God, Jesus, the church?

In what ways might this church be similar to and different from other Christian churches?

To make this easier and perhaps more practical, perhaps you could pick one other church and compare yours to it OR if you are not associated with an organized church compare your view of following Jesus with the way some organized Christian religious group might view it.

Christian churches, over time, have developed a set of beliefs about many topics. These beliefs are found in statements of faith and in creeds, often found in the church's worship books and the hymnals you will find that they use when they worship. Some churches (ex: Presbyterians, Lutherans, Roman Catholics and others) have catechisms in which the basic principles of Christian faith as they interpret it are stated. Some Christian churches see the beliefs in these catechisms as more binding on the consciences of the believer than others do. These catechisms or statements of faith as some organized Christian groups call them identify how the church sees certain important topics. Here are some typical questions these church documents explore:

Who is God?

Who is Jesus?

What is the church?

What is the meaning of the sacraments? (Different churches view the NUMBER of sacraments differently and may even define the term differently)

How are we to pray?

How does one live as a Christian in the world?

What do we believe after the afterlife?

What teachings are ESSENTIAL to our faith?

Where does the Bible fit into the faith and practice of individuals in this church?

Under this umbrella, you will see that certain churches are inspired by great thinkers and leaders who have been part of that tradition, some inspiring both Protestants and Catholics, although with different points of emphasis. An example would be Augustine. For Methodists, John Wesley would have great influence. Lutherans look to Luther, Reformed churches to John Calvin... and on and on... Likewise, organized churches have been responsible for building all kinds of institutions that are part of many societies-colleges, hospitals, social service agencies, homes for the elderly, etc. If you look up the historical background of American colleges and universities, you will find LARGE numbers of them were founded by varied churches.

Over the course of history, some have questioned whether it is possible to be Christian without being part of a church. In the most fundamental sense, a Christian is nothing more than one who seeks to follow Jesus. In the process of following Jesus, we learn, however, that Jesus INTENTIONALLY called and gathered followers (disciples) and intended them to gather and continue His mission even after he no longer walked the face of the earth. Therefore, there seems to be a clear connection between the MISSION of Jesus and a COMMUNITY which would seek to live out His mission.

As you consider this and possibly discuss this in your setting or with others, I ask that you consider the following:

If you are a member of a church or studying in a church group, explore and discuss the influence of one of your church's historic leaders and thinkers on the life of the church (ex: Luther, Wesley, Calvin, Aquinas or others in whose direction your group leader can point you)

Where would you look to find the 'teachings' of your church?

Give your opinion: Do you need to be part of a church to be a Christian?

Give your opinion: Is Christianity possible without the church?

Identify the following:

a. Some good things 'organized religion' has done throughout history.
b. Some bad things 'organized religion' has done throughout history.

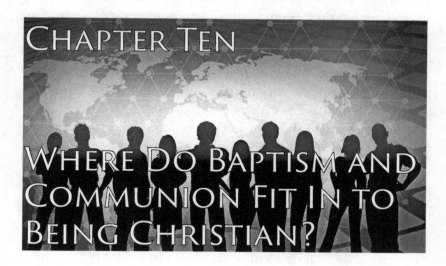

CHAPTER TEN

WHERE DO BAPTISM AND COMMUNION FIT IN TO BEING CHRISTIAN?

I f you are part of a church or learning about a church, you will have experienced or discovered that there are certain official ritual actions that are part of this religious community of which you have been part or about which you are learning. These rituals include the following:

People get together for worship. Most Christian churches have Sunday set aside as the day of worship. Some others worship on Saturday.

At worship, people often share Holy Communion. Some churches do this weekly. Others once a month. Still some others, less often.

People are baptized. They become part of the community. Most Christian churches make Baptism available to infants. Others practice what is known as 'believer's Baptism,' i.e. you are baptized when you are able to profess your faith in Jesus on your own.

As part of the church's life, people participate in other rituals. Some churches have Confirmation or offer Anointing for Healing. Some have special rituals associated with the time of death. Churches have organized ways to ordain, install, choose and affirm their pastors and other leaders. Churches offer opportunities for couples to be married within the context of a ritual containing prayer and blessing. Within church communities, people confess their sins and are assured of God's forgiveness. Many churches do so through prayers people pray together at worship. Some churches offer opportunities for private, personal confession.

Many Christian communities call some of these ritual actions SACRAMENTS. Others prefer the term ORDINANCE. The Roman Catholic Church accepts the following as Sacraments: Baptism, Confirmation, Eucharist, Marriage, Reconciliation, Holy Orders, Anointing of the Sick. Protestants who use the term sacrament tend to identify two — Baptism and Eucharist, while acknowledging the importance of the others as ritual actions.

The history of sacraments in the church is a lengthy one. Fortunately, most Christian churches see the value in a wide variety of prayer and ritual opportunities, while often differing on what they call them or whether they were directly intended by Jesus. While some Christians differ on the age or method of Baptism and Communion and while there is difference among Christians regarding the meaning of Communion, there IS unity of thought that these actions of BAPTISM and COMMUNION should be a central part of the life of the church.

In BAPTISM, one becomes a Christian. Those churches that baptize infants see Confirmation as an affirmation of Baptism and also build in to regular worship services opportunities to reflect on and renew Baptism. Many churches have Baptismal fonts located in prominent places and as part of the prayers associated with different seasons provide people the opportunity to be sprinkled with Baptismal water. In COMMUNION, churches celebrate their unity in Jesus and follow His directive to 'Do this in memory of me,' words he stated at the last supper meal.

Over the course of history, there have been significant differences among Christian churches about what happens at Communion. The traditional Roman Catholic position has been that the bread and wine of Communion really becomes the Body and Blood of Christ. Many other Christians hold a different position emphasizing less a physical change while still saying that Christ is present under the appearance of bread and wine, the bread and wine remaining exactly that. Still others insist that a service of Communion is essentially a service of REMEMBERING what Jesus has done.

I can't help inserting an opinion here: I think there has been too much division on this topic of Communion in the life of the church and I think churches need to find ways to bring each other together at table. Some would disagree with me for sure, insisting that in suggesting this, I am watering down a truth of our faith. I don't believe that I am. Instead, I encourage you to consider this:

I believe that when you come to celebrate a service at which Communion is a part, Jesus Christ is truly present in YOU and in those gathered around:

Christ is present is EVERYONE because He is who He is

Those gathered will include the baptized who have accepted the gift of their baptism and see themselves as disciples of Jesus.

Christ is present in the words of scripture that are read and that fill the service, pointing us as worshipers to him

Christ is present in the act of sharing this meal IN REMEM-BRANCE OF HIM who also happens to be VERY PRESENT.

What I am saying is that at certain points in history, people emphasized certain insights about what happens at Communion, each of which definitely has made a contribution, yet individually have not always seen the big picture.

For those such as I who like to use the word SACRAMENT, I find this explanation of a sacrament to make particular sense: A sacrament is a SIGN that CAUSES that which it signifies.

Applied to Baptism, the pouring of water symbolizes our connection as individuals with the death and eternal life of Jesus while, at the same time, causing us to move forward in a faith that, even out of suffering and death, comes life. In terms of Communion, the sharing of bread and wine, while being an outward sign of our unity in Christ, actually helps to make the bonds even deeper.

I love these words of a popular Communion hymn, "Draw us in the Spirit's Tether":

All our meals and all our living make as sacraments of you
That by loving, caring, giving, we may be disciples true
Alleluia, Alleluia, we may serve with faith anew.

WHAT DO YOU THINK? Whether you are reading this book on your own or in a class, please consider these questions:

QUESTIONS FOR DISCUSSION:

1.   Have you been baptized? When? How would you describe the difference it makes in your life, if any?
2.   What does Communion mean to you?
3.   If you are in a class associated with a church:
     a.   Research your church/denomination teaching on Communion
     b.   Look at that teaching and discuss your opinion of it
     c.   Research the position of a Christian church other than your own and be prepared to explain it in its own terms.

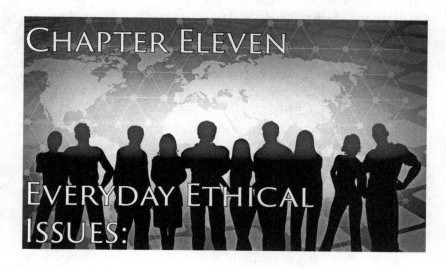

CHAPTER ELEVEN

EVERYDAY ETHICAL ISSUES:

HOW MIGHT FAITH IN JESUS INFLUENCE THE DECISIONS I MAKE?

There are a lot of people who, when observing all of the differences that people who call themselves religious have with each other, make the argument that what is more important than what people think about religious matters is the way that they act. Oftentimes, this reaction is inspired by the way that the expression of religious conviction often crosses the line into nastiness and outright meanness. While I do happen to believe that how you think is important, very important, in fact, I appreciate and agree with the underlying conviction that what is really important is how we live and how we treat each other!

Now, believing as I do, that how you think IS important, what I want to do in this chapter is to consider how one's faith in Jesus might make a difference in the kinds of decisions we have to make in our lives that we might call ethical (or moral decisions, i.e. decisions of what is right and what is wrong.) My point to you is a simple one: That if you believe that Jesus is worth following because of what you believe ABOUT him, as I do, then it is really important to look at what he has to say which might be helpful in terms of helping you shape how you make concrete decisions about the situations in your life.

Please understand: I am not saying that you can open your Bible and find the answer to every ethical question you have. I am also not saying that the Bible, in which you read about what Jesus said, tackles some of the everyday questions that face you in this, the 21st century. I am most certainly not making the point that God expects us not to think through ethical questions. We are not robots. One could argue that we would not have been given a brain and a conscience to decide right from wrong if it were not a wise thing for us to do our best to use it.

What I am saying is that while you can't look up in a book what Jesus actually would say about war, peace, immigration, gay rights, health care or any other 'hot button' political issue, you can read the teachings of Jesus and get a clear sense of his values. These values can then form our conscience and lead us to make concrete decisions about the direction of our lives.

Of course, it is very possible that we could be struggling with two different values that are both based on Christian principles. Here I would like to tell you something about an amazing Christian writer and thinker by the name of Dietrich Bonhoeffer. Bonhoeffer was a German who lived during World War II. As a follower of Jesus and a pastor, he was deeply disturbed by what Hitler was doing to the Jewish people during this horrible time which we identify as the Holocaust. As a committed Christian, Bonhoeffer believed that all human beings are created in God's image and that killing was not a positive Christian value. It was something to be avoided.

Yet, Bonhoeffer also knew that Hitler, responsible for the death of so many innocents, needed to be stopped. He had conversations with many Hitler opponents and was implicated by the authorities in a conspiracy to assassinate Hitler. Some Christians would argue that he was wrong to even consider the act of murder. After all, didn't Jesus really advocate nonviolence? But others would say that if Bonhoeffer's purpose was to stop an evil man from killing thousands of more innocent people, then perhaps there IS a moral ground to be involved in such a conspiracy. The history of Christianity is filled with discussion, disagreement and debate about whether the ends can ever justify the means, whether situation ethics, as it is called, can ever really be Christian ethics or whether it is really possible to distinguish, as to many, killing from the act of murder.

My point is that this is really not clear cut and that Jesus did not provide an answer guide to all moral dilemmas. Instead, I look at it this way: If you read the Gospels and look at WHAT Jesus said and HOW he treated others, it is hard to argue against these points:

Jesus taught that we are ALL children of God

He taught LOVE of all, including enemies

He stood up for those who were considered outsiders

He treated women with a respect not often found in the patriarchical society in which he lived

He emphasized forgiveness

He practiced nonviolence, even to the point of death, where He himself was a victim of capital punishment

He did not isolate or ostracize 'the sinner'

In my opinion, some oversimplify this by saying that Jesus taught us all simply 'to be nice and to be good.' The fact is that Jesus was very firm in his criticism of those who did NOT treat people as the daughters and sons of God whom they were. The fact also is that living out Christian faith, as Jesus taught, can come at a considerable cost. My encouragement to you is that you take some time to read about the lives of these individuals who are part of fairly contemporary Christian history who I list in a text box earlier on: Bonhoeffer, Martin Luther King, Dorothy Day, Oscar Romero. In all of their lives, you will see that there are times when living out a 'Christian ethic' might require that one pay a great price….and I am not talking about money!

We can also say of Jesus that he said nothing directly about some of the issues that divide Christians because the questions we have about these issues just were not around at the time. Contemporary issues of gender identity, abortion, orientation, climate change and several other matters were not part of the conversation in Jesus' day.

With respect to the last example, what we are really left with is trying our very best to examine the spirit that drove Jesus to teach what he taught and to try to apply that spirit to these issues about which he did not speak directly.

In looking at climate change as one example, while it was a non issue in Jesus' day, we can say with certainty that Jesus, as a faithful Jewish believer, had deep regard and respect for all of creation as a gift from God. From that underlying principle, one can draw inspiration in making certain specific moral decisions. While the Bible does not deal explicitly with every possible question of sexual morality, it is clear that Jesus would have a serious problem with unfaithfulness (as he did) or with using another for the purpose of having one's sexual needs met.

There are a wide variety of issues in which people of good faith can differ on specific ethical decisions. In thinking over my own life, as someone who lived during the Vietnam era, I was deeply opposed to the war in Vietnam on moral grounds, based on the teachings of Jesus. While I still do not agree with the positions of those who supported the war, I have come to understand that many who did so were doing their very best to try to do what is right and to put into practice their Christian conviction.

As you discuss or think about this chapter, I ask you to do the following:

Identify FIVE complicated moral issues.

Using your understanding of Jesus' teachings, how would you apply those teachings to how you would deal with those issues?

What would be great is if you could have good, serious conversation that would emerge from your attempt to grapple with these questions. I use the word 'grapple' intentionally. We are human beings, not God. We do not know everything. As we go through life, we recognize that our knowledge is limited. So, what we need to do is to be honest and sincere and to really try our best to do what is right.

In my life, because of my personal belief in who Jesus is and who he is for me, the greatest part of doing what is right is attempting to take his values and teachings and apply them to the concrete decisions that we have to make. It is not always easy. What appears to be absolute in the abstract is often ambiguous in the concrete situation. Don't let that discourage you. My personal opinion is: Keep your eyes on Jesus, dig deeply into the spirit and intent of Jesus' words and life, do so sincerely, dialogue with others who seek to do what is right as well, do your very best and know that you are deeply loved by a God who created you and all the world and who, in the fullness of time, lived through the words and life and death … and life … of Jesus!

BONUS QUESTIONS FOR DISCUSSION OR SIMPLY SOME THOUGHT…

What do you make of that statement above: 'What appears to be absolute in the abstract is often ambiguous in the concrete situation?' What might that possibly mean? Explain abstract and concrete in theeh context of the question. Give examples.

Discuss that final phrase of mine… About God who 'In the fullness of time lived through the words and life and death…and life…of Jesus?' What does this phrase mean to you?

CONCLUSION

I have written this little book to be read by you at this moment of your life, this time of adolescence with all of its unique developmental tasks and challenges. In writing it, I recognized that you might have just picked this up and read it on your own because you saw its title somewhere or you were reading and discussing it as part of a group, such as a class.

Whatever the context is, I hope you have found it to be of value at this point in your life. Even though it is really written for teenagers, I also hope that maybe someday in the distant future, you will pick it up again, even though by that point, you will have found other books that speak to your life experiences at that particular point in time and your teenage years may even seem to you as of a lifetime ago.

I will end with a prayer that has meant a lot to me from the time i first heard it. As you seek to navigate YOUR way through the mysteries of your own life, I hope you find it meaningful to you as well. This is a prayer written by Thomas Merton, a man about whom I would most definitely suggest you do some reading sometime:

"My Lord God, I have no idea where I am going. I do not see the road ahead of me. I cannot know for certain where it will end. Nor do I really know myself, and the fact that I think that I am following your will does not mean that I am actually doing so. But I believe that the desire to please you does in fact please you. And I hope I have that desire in all that I am doing. I hope that I will never do anything apart from that desire. And I know that if I do this you will lead me by the right road, though I may know nothing about it. Therefore will I trust you always, though I may seem to be lost and in the shadow of death. I will not fear, for you are ever with me, and you will never leave me to face my perils alone."

SUGGESTIONS FOR FURTHER EXPLORATION

As you read this book on your own or in a class setting, you may find you would like to explore some of the topics discussed here in more detail. Here are a few suggestions:

BIBLE

I recommend a Bible with good, updated footnotes. I strongly suggest the New Revised Standard Version. Roman Catholic readers will benefit from the excellent translation of the New American Bible. Those in the Lutheran tradition might want to explore the *Lutheran Study Bible*. In addition, *The Message* is an excellent work which presents the Bible in contemporary language. I do not suggest it as a substitute for the other Bibles, but as a good supplementary resource.

VIDEOS

I suggest these films: *Luther, Romero, Gandhi, A Rose in December* (a PBS special about Jean Donovan, an American murdered in El Salvador) and the PBS special *Bonhoeffer*. As a starting point, Wikipedia is a good place to get started reading about Dorothy Day, Cesar Chavez, and Dietrich Bonhoeffer. Reading as much as possible about the life and original writings of Dr. Martin Luther King would be of great value as well. Videos of his speeches are available on YouTube. It would be great to explore the religious basis of his writings. The works of former President Jimmy Carter are worth exploring as well. They provide many insights into applying Christian faith to real life issues.

CATECHISMS

You may want to explore the catechisms of at least TWO different Christian churches, one being your own if you are part of a church community.

OTHER RESOURCES

For a great overview of the importance of understanding religion in the modern world, take a look at Stephen Prothero's *Religious Literacy*. If you are interested in a fairly contemporary autobiographical exploration of religious questions and different churches, you may want to take a peek at my book, *Crossing the Street*.

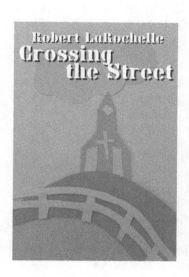
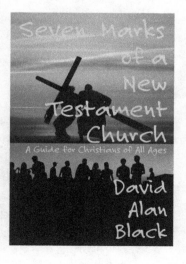

MORE FROM ENERGION PUBLICATIONS

Personal Study

When People Speak for God	Henry Neufeld	$17.99
The Sacred Journey	Chris Surber	$11.99
It's in the Bag	Kimberly Gordon	$5.99
It's in the Toolbox	Greg May	$5.99

Devotions

Daily Devotions of Ordinary People	Jody Neufeld	$19.99
Crewed Awakening	Greg May	$19.99
Good Morning, Lord!	Linda Estes	$12.99
Assenting to the Eternal	Carolyn Côté	$9.99

Bible Study

Learning and Living Scripture	Lentz/Neufeld	$12.99
Luke: A Participatory Study Guide	Geoffrey Lentz	$9.99
Galatians: A Participatory Study Guide	Bruce Epperly	$12.99
Colossians & Philemon	Allan Bevere	$12.99
Creation in Scripture	Herold Weiss	$12.99
Ruth & Esther	Bruce Epperly	$5.99
Who's Afraid of the Old Testament God?	Alden Thompson	$14.99

Prayer

Pathways to Prayer	David Moffett-Moore	$5.99
Jonah: When God Changes	Bruce Epperly	$5.99
Ultimate Allegiance	Bob Cornwall	$9.99

Fiction

The Traveler's Advance	Heath Taws	$13.99
Megabelt	Nick May	$12.99
Prayer Trilogy	Kimberly Gordon	$9.99

Poetry

noise flash	Lee Baker	$14.99
Poetic Diversities	Tabitha Edwards-Walton	$9.99

Generous Quantity Discounts Available

Dealer Inquiries Welcome

Energion Publications — P.O. Box 841

Gonzalez, FL_ 32560

Website: http://energionpubs.com

Phone: (850) 525-3916

CPSIA information can be obtained
at www.ICGtesting.com
Printed in the USA
LVHW010838280121
677609LV00006B/684